I was eight years old that year.

Each day of the summer holidays,

I wrote one sentence in my notebook:

one thing that had happened to me.

That was my assignment from school,

the condition for moving on to the next year.

I still have the notebook.

15.7.1939

I walked to the brook with my
brother and our nanny.

16.7.1939

I went to church.

A young girl arrived at the guesthouse
where I'm staying.

18.7.1939

I went to the woods with a friend.

19.7.1939

I went to Wawer to say goodbye to Mummy.

21.7.1939

I went for a walk with Grandma.

23.7.1939

I found a big caterpillar and brought it
to our garden.

15. III. 1939.

Byłem z bratem i z wycho-
wawczynią nad potokiem.

16. III. 1939.

Byłem w kościele.

17. III. 1939.

Do tego pensjonatu w
którym mieszkam przyje-
chała mała dziewczynka.

15.7.1939
I walked to the brook with my brother
and our nanny.

16.7.1939
I went to church.

17.7.1939
A young girl arrived at the guesthouse
where I'm staying.

18. 7. 1939. r.

Byłem z kolegą w lesie.

19. 7 1939 r.

Odprowadziłem ma

musie do Wawra.

20. 7. 1939 r

Wysłałem zyczenia

imeninowe dla kuzynka

21. 7. 1939 r

Byłem z babcią na spacerze.

18.7.1939
I went to the woods with a friend.

19.7.1939
I went to Wawer to say goodbye to Mummy.

20.7.1939
I sent a name day card to my cousin.

21.7.1939
I went for a walk with Grandma.

22. 7 1939 r

Byłem w kasynie na lodach.

23. 7 1939r

Znalazłem dużą liszkę i
zaniłem do swego ogródka.

24. 7 1939 r

Bawiłem się w piasku i
budowałem z pia niego
most.

22.7.1939
I had ice cream at a casino.

23.7.1939
I found a big caterpillar and brought it
to our garden.

24.7.1939
I played in the sand and
built a sand castle.

25.7.1939

There was a terrible storm.

A plane circled over Anin.

27.7.1939

I went for a ride in a car.

28.7.1939

I saw a beautiful woodpecker.

29.7.1939

The power in Anin went out.

30.7.1939

A hot-air balloon flew over Anin.

25. 7 1939 r

Była straszna burza.

26. 7 1939 r

Nad Aninem krążył
samolot.

27. 7 1939

Byłem samochodem na
wycieczce.

25.7.1939
There was a terrible storm.

26.7.1939
A plane circled over Anin.

27.7.1939
I went for a ride in a car.

28.7.1939.

Widziałem pięknego

dzięcioła.

29.7.1939

W Aninie zyskła elektry-

czność.

30.7.1939 r

Nad Aninem leciał balon.

28.7.1939
I saw a beautiful woodpecker.

29.7.1939
The power in Anin went out.

30.7.1939
A hot-air balloon flew over Anin.

31.7.1939

A plane towing a glider flew over Anin.

2.8.1939

I'm waiting for Mummy to arrive.

3.8.1939

I went to Anin railway station.

4.8.1939

I went to Wawer railway station twice.

31. 7. 1939. r.

Nad Aninem samolot na-
ciągał szybowca.

1. 8. 1939. r

Przyjechała do mnie bab-
cia.

2. 8. 1939. r.

Czekam na przyjazd

mamusi.

31.7.1939
A plane towing a glider flew over Anin.

1.8.1939
Grandma came to see me.

2.8.1939
I'm waiting for Mummy to arrive.

3.8.1939. r.

Byłem na stacji Anin.

4.8.1939 r.

Byłem 2 razy na stacji
Wawer.

5.8.1939. r.

Przyjechał do mnie dzia=
dziuś.

3.8.1939
I went to Anin railway station.

4.8.1939
I went to Wawer railway station twice.

5.8.1939
Grandpa came to see me.

6.8.1939

I went in a car to the Miłosna district.

7.8.1939

I caught a wasp in a glass.

8.8.1939

Our housekeeper came.

9.8.1939

Two storms passed through Anin.

11.8.1939

I went with Daddy for a fun walk.

6. 8. 1939 r

Pojechałem autem do Mi =

łosnej.

7. 8. 1939 r.

Złapałem osę do szklan

ki.

8. 8. 1939 r.

Przyjechała do mnie gosposia

9.8.1939 r.

Nad Aninem przeszły
2 burze.

10.8.1939 r.

Oglądałem bajkę. o 3
świnkach.

11.8.1939 r.

Byłem z tatusiem na
wesołym spacerze.

9.8.1939
Two storms passed through Anin.

10.8.1939
I watched a story about three pigs.

11.8.1939
I went with Daddy for a fun walk.

12.8.1939

My brother fell ill.

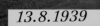

13.8.1939

I went for a walk with Grandpa.

15.8.1939

I arrived in Warsaw.

18.8.1939

I played football.

12.8.1939. r.

zachorował mój Brat.

13.8.1939. r.

Byłem z dziadziusiem na

spacerze.

14.8.1939. r.

Bawiłem się w lotto

15.8.1939. r.

Przyjechałem do Warsza =

12.8.1939
My brother fell ill.

14.8.1939
I played a game of lotto.

13.8.1939
I went for a walk with Grandpa.

15.8.1939
I arrived in Warsaw.

wy.

16.8.1939.r.

Z Anina przywiozłem 2

kwiatki.

17.8.1939.r

Byłem z babcią na spa =

cerze.

18.8.1939.r.

Bawiłem się piłką nożną.

16.8.1939
I brought back two flowers from Anin.

17.8.1939
I went for a walk with Grandma.

18.8.1939
I played football.

19.8.1939

I am going with Grandma to Jabłkowskis'.

20.8.1939

I came to Grandma's house.

21.8.1939

I worked with Grandma in the garden.

23.8.1939

I had ice cream at a patisserie.

19. 8. 1939. r.

Pójdę z babcią do Jabłkow-
skich.

20. 8. 1939. r.

Przyjechałem do babci.

21. 8. 1939. r.

Pracowałem z babcią w
ogródku.

19.8.1939
I am going with Grandma to Jabłkowskis'.

20.8.1939
I came to Grandma's house.

21.8.1939
I worked with Grandma in the garden.

22.8.1939. r.

Byłem u babci i zrobiłem

most.

23.8.1939. r.

Byłem w cukierni na

lodach.

24.8.1939. r.

Bawiłem się z bratem w

ping-ponga.

22.8.1939
I built a bridge at Grandma's.

23.8.1939
I had ice cream at a patisserie.

24.8.1939
I played table tennis with my brother.

25.8.1939

I read a nice story.

27.8.1939

I went to Żeromski Park.

28.8.1939

I watered the garden with a hose.

29.8.1939

Daddy came to visit me.

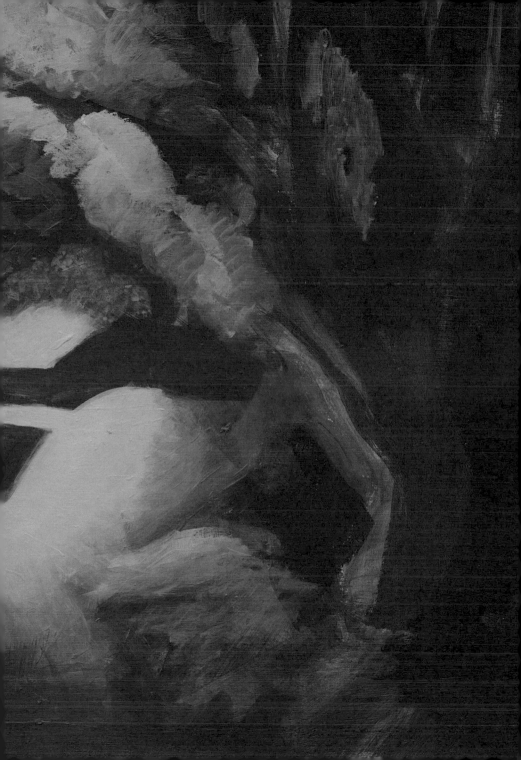

30.8.1939

I played with Magdusia.

25. 8. 1939. r.

Czytałem ładną bajkę.

26. 8. 1939. r.

Byłem w cukierni na

lodach.

27. 8. 1939. r.

Byłem w parku Że =

romskiega.

25.8.1939
I read a nice story.

26.8.1939
I had ice cream at a patisserie.

27.8.1939
I went to Żeromski Park.

28.8.1939. r.

Podlewałem ogród

z węża.

29.8.1939. r.

Odwiedził mnie tatuś

30.8.1939. r.

Bawiłem się z Mag =

dusią.

28.8.1939
I watered the garden with a hose.

29.8.1939
Daddy came to visit me.

30.8.1939
I played with Magdusia.

31.8.1939

My nanny came to see me.

1.9.1939

The war began.

2.9.1939

I arrived in Milanówek.

3.9.1939

I was hiding from the planes.

4.9.1939

Aunt and Auntie came.

5.9.1939

Grandpa came to see me.

31.8.1939. r.

Przyjjechała do mnie bona.

1.9.1939. r.

Rozpoczęta się wojna.

2.9.1939. r.

Przyjjechałem do Mi = lanówka.

31.8.1939
My nanny came to see me.

1.9.1939
The war began.

2.9.1939
I arrived in Milanówek.

3. 9. 1939. r.

O Chowałem się przed
tot samolotami.

4. 9. 1939. r.

Przyjechali do mnie

ciocia i wujek.

5. 9. 1939. r.

Przyjechał do mnie.

dziadziuś.

3.9.1939
I was hiding from the planes.

4.9.1939
Aunt and Auntie came.

5.9.1939
Grandpa came to see me.

6.9.1939

They dropped a bomb near us.

7.9.1939

The Germans captured Milanówek.

9.9.1939

Planes keep flying overhead.

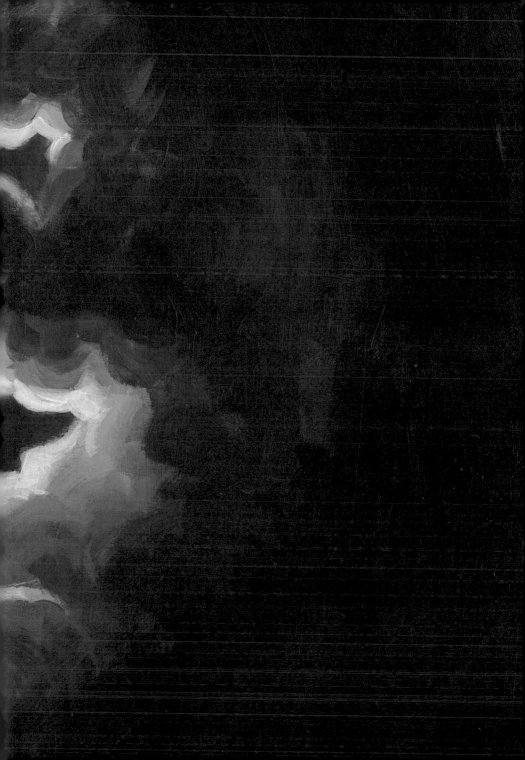

10.9.1939

There's going to be a terrible fight.

11.9.1939

We can hear cannon blasts.

12.9.1939

Shrapnel flew over our house.

14.9.1939

Warsaw is defending itself bravely.

6.9.1939. r.

Rzucali bliżej blizko.
nasz bombę.
7.9.1939 r.
Niemcy zajęli Mila =
nówek.
8.9.1939. r.
Karmiłem kury i kurczę
ta.

6.9.1939
They dropped a bomb near us.

7.9.1939
The Germans captured Milanówek.

8.9.1939
I fed the chicks and chickens.

9.9.1939.r

Stale latają samoloty

10.9.1939.r.

Ma być okropny bój

11.9.1939.r.

Słychać strzały armat=

nie

12.9.1939.r.

Te przeleciały nad naszym

9.9.1939
Planes keep flying overhead.

10.9.1939
There's going to be a terrible fight.

11.9.1939
We can hear cannon blasts.

12.9.1939
Shrapnel flew over our house.

domem szrapnele.

13.9.1939. r.

Zaczęli wydawać chleb na
kartki.

14.9.1939. r.

Warszawa się dzielnie
broni

15.9.1939.

Samolot angielski

13.9.1939
They started rationing bread.

14.9.1939
Warsaw is defending itself bravely.

15.9.1939
An English plane dropped three bombs
on the German Army.

rzucił 3 bąby na woj =
sko niemieckie.
19. 16. 9. 1939. r.
17. 9. 1939. r.

About the Book

The author of the notebook on which this book is based is still alive. In 1939, he lived with his parents and younger brother in the Mokotów district of Warsaw. That year, he was spending the summer holidays with his brother in the care of their nanny, who after a while was relieved by their grandmother. After staying at a guesthouse in Anin (a residential area in the Wawer district, then adjacent to Warsaw), followed by several days at his family home, he went to stay with his grandparents at their house with a garden in the Żoliborz district. After the war broke out, the boys' grandfather took them to their great-grandfather's house in Milanówek (a town about 30 km southwest of today's Warsaw), where they stayed with their grandmother.

In each of these places, eight-year-old Michał wrote one sentence a day in his notebook. That very notebook has been reproduced in its entirety within this book. Most entries have also been replicated in text on the illustrated pages, with the translated text using corrected and standardised spelling.

The sentence dated 29 August records the author's last meeting with his father. His father was a pilot and leader of a bomber squadron. He lost his life on 9 September 1939 in a plane crash.

The last sentence of the notebook – which is not accompanied by an illustration – probably repeats rumours that were circulating at the time and is not historically accurate. It does convey, however, the prevailing mood in the country and the widespread faith in British support.

The "Jabłkowskis'" mentioned in the text refers to the Jabłkowski Brothers department store on Bracka Street in Warsaw. Magdusia was the author's cousin. Miłosna likely refers to today's residential area of Stara Miłosna in Warsaw's Wesoła district. Żeromski Park is also located in Warsaw.

Originally published in 2019 by Dwie Siostry under the title
Widziałem pięknego dzięcioła
© text: Marcin Skibiński, 2019
© illustrations: Ala Bankroft, 2019
English translation © Eliza Marciniak

© for the English edition: 2021, Prestel Verlag,
Munich · London · New York
A member of Penguin Random House Verlagsgruppe GmbH
Neumarkter Strasse 28 · 81673 Munich

Translated from the Polish by Eliza Marciniak

Library of Congress Control Number: 2021933405
A CIP catalogue record for this book is available
from the British Library.

Editorial direction: Doris Kutschbach
Project management: Constanze Holler
Copyediting: Ayesha Wadhawan
Design and layout: Ewa Stiasny
Production management and typesetting: Susanne Hermann
Separations: Reproline Mediateam
Printing and binding: DZS Grafik, d.o.o., Slovenia

This book has been published
with the support of the ©POLAND
Translation Program

Our production is
climate neutral
ClimatePartner.com/14044-1912-1001
Print product

Prestel Publishing compensates the CO$_2$ emissions
produced from the making of this book by
supporting a reforestation project in Brazil.
Find further information on the project here:
www.ClimatePartner.com/14044-1912-1001

MIX
Paper from
responsible sources
FSC® C106600

Penguin Random House Verlagsgruppe
FSC® N001967
ISBN 978-3-7913-7486-4

www.prestel.com